D0966521

A Gift For:

Kristin

From:

Gena

MADE IT

a photographic celebration

BOK3049

Action springs not

from thought, but

from a readiness

for responsibility.

Dietrich Bonhoeffer

BRASIL

Every great man is unique.

Ralph Waldo Emerson

To travel hopefully is a better thing than to arrive, and the true success is to labor.

Robert L. Stevenson

Obstacles cannot crush me.

Every obstacle yields to

stern resolve. He who is

fixed to a star does not

change his mind.

Leonardo da Vinci

Don't ever take a fence

down until you know

why it was put up.

Robert Frost

Amazing what you can do when

you put your mind to it.

Anonymous

?MARK

Do not go where the path

may lead, go instead

where there is no path and

leave a trail.

Ralph Waldo Emerson

If you can't convince them, confuse them.

Harry S Truman

The important thing is not to stop questioning. Curiosity has its own reason for existing. One cannot help but be in awe when he contemplates the mysteries of eternity, of life, of the marvelous structure of reality. It is enough if one tries merely to comprehend a little of this mystery every day. Never lose a holy curiosity.

Albert Einstein

The optimist sees

opportunity in every

danger; the pessimist

sees danger in every

opportunity.

Winston Churchill

STRAND FLEET ST
CANNON STREET

Genius is 99 percent perspiration

and 1 percent inspiration.

Thomas Edison

What does not kill me

makes me stronger.

Johann Wolfgang von Goethe

WINNER
PUP OF THE YEAR

There is one quality which one must possess to win, and that is definiteness of purpose, the knowledge of what one wants, and a burning desire to possess it.

Napoleon Hill

You cannot create experience.

You must undergo it.

Albert Camus

Now, here, you see, it takes all the running you can do, to keep in the same place. If you want to get somewhere else, you must run at least twice as fast as that!

Lewis Carroll

You are a human boy, my young friend.

A human boy.

O glorious to be a human boy!

O running stream of sparkling joy

To be a soaring human boy!

Charles Dickens

Always do right; this will gratify some

people and astonish the rest.

Mark Twain

Victory belongs to the most persevering.

Napoleon Bonaparte

DONNAY
DONNAY

Success is never final.

Failure is never fatal.

It is courage that counts.

Winston Churchill

If, at first, you do succeed,

try to hide your astonishment.

Los Angeles Times

Moderation is a fatal thing.

Nothing succeeds like excess.

Oscar Wilde

Whether you think that you can, or

that you can't, you are usually right.

Henry Ford

There can only be one state of

mind as you approach any

profound test; total

concentration, a spirit of

togetherness, and strength.

Pat Riley

Every calling is great when greatly pursued.

Oliver Wendell Holmes

Don't bother just to be better than your

contemporaries or predecessors.

Try to be better than yourself.

William Faulkner

Happiness makes up in

height for what it lacks

in length.

Robert Frost

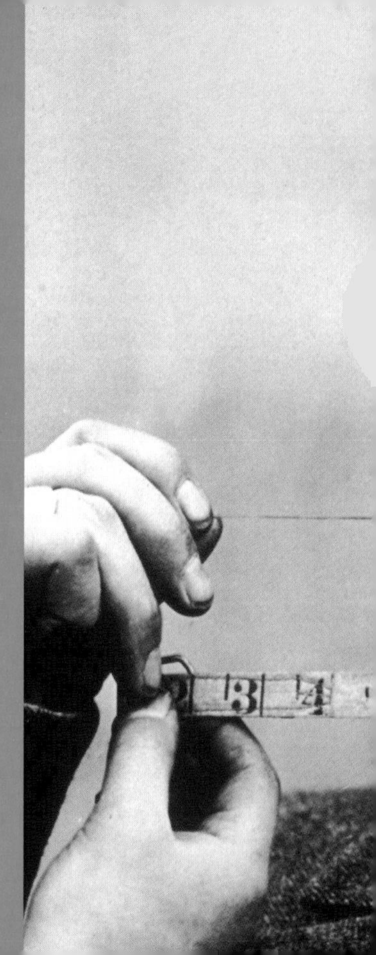

If you have built castles in the air,

your work need not be lost; that is

where they should be. Now put

the foundations under them.

Henry David Thoreau

No bird soars too high if he
soars with his own wings.

William Blake

AAU
USA

Glory gives herself only to those who

always dreamed of her.

Charles de Gaulle

The great and glorious

masterpiece of humanity is to

know how to live with a purpose.

Michel de Montaigne

Concentration is the secret of strength.

Ralph Waldo Emerson

Experience is one thing

you can't get for nothing.

Oscar Wilde

Pleasure in the job puts perfection in the work.

Aristotle

Whatever you can do or dream

you can, begin it. Boldness has

genius, power, and magic in it.

Johann Wolfgang von Goethe

He that would have the fruit must climb the tree.

Thomas Fuller, M.D.

BUROHAU

Shoot for the moon.

Even if you miss, you'll land among the stars.

Les Brown

On matters of style, swim with the current,

on matters of principle, stand like a rock.

Thomas Jefferson

Confidence is preparation. Everything else is beyond your control.

Richard Kline

People rarely succeed unless they have fun in what they are doing.

Dale Carnegie

ESCAPE
PANEL

Nothing great was ever

achieved without enthusiasm.

Ralph Waldo Emerson

Be like a postage stamp.

Stick to one thing until

you get there.

Josh Billings

Always bear in mind that

your own resolution to

success is more important

than any other one thing.

Abraham Lincoln

A really great talent finds its

happiness in execution.

Johann Wolfgang von Goethe

8
9

When you've done the best you can, you can't do any better.

Harry S Truman

Minds are like parachutes—

they only function when open.

Thomas Dewar

Whatever you are, be a good one.

Abraham Lincoln

Life is a series of experiences, each

one of which makes us bigger...

Henry Ford

We act as though comfort and luxury were the chief requirements in life, when all that we need to make us really happy is something to be enthusiastic about.

Charles Kingsley

How you respond to the challenge in the second half will determine what you become after the game, whether you are a winner or not.

Lou Holtz

Keep away from people who try to

belittle your ambitions. Small

people always do that, but the

really great make you feel that

you, too, can become great.

Mark Twain

There comes that mysterious

meeting in life when

someone acknowledges who

we are and what we can be,

igniting the circuits of our

highest potential.

Rusty Berkus

One can never consent to creep

when one feels an impulse to soar.

Helen Keller

One of the greatest discoveries a man makes, one of his great surprises, is to find he can do what he was afraid he couldn't do.

Henry Ford

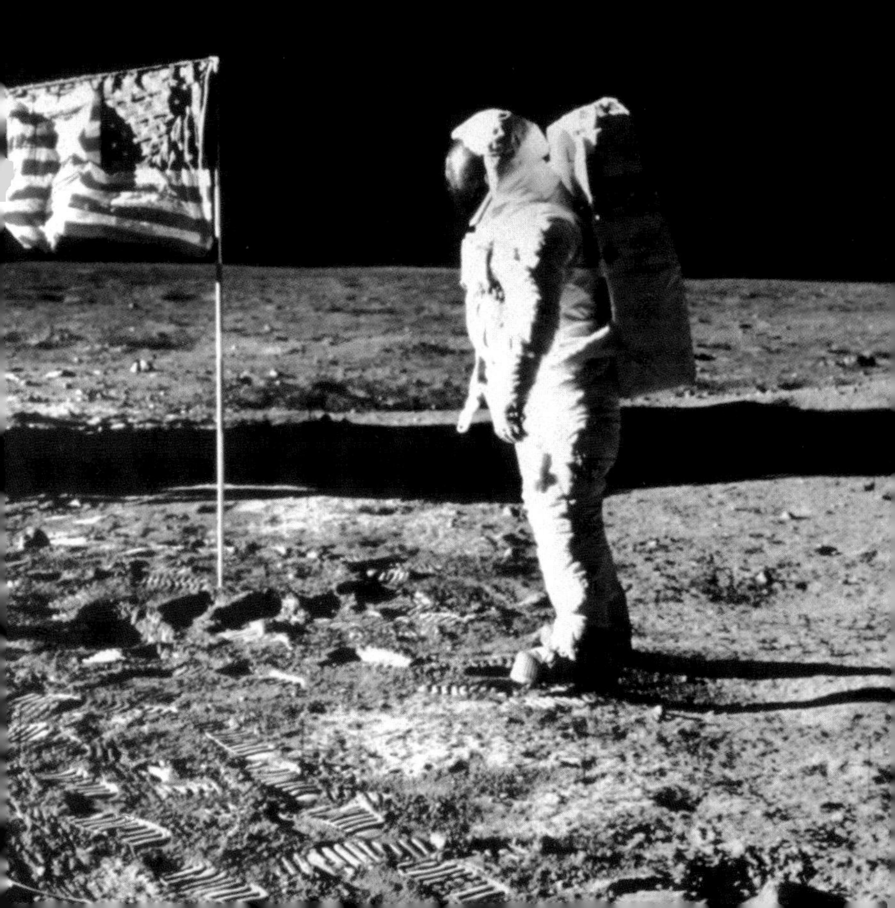

Picture Credits

All images Hulton Getty Picture Collection, unless otherwise specified.

cover: A man balances on the peak of a mountain, circa 1980.

title page: Janet Jeffreys practices her long jump, 1954.

page 5: Gilmar, Brazil's national team goalkeeper saves a goal before a match with the English side, 1956.

page 6: Playing a game of leap frog outdoors, © Lambert/Hulton Archive, circa 1955.

page 9: Farmer Colin Newlove and his Yorkshire bull jump through a burning hoop, 1963.

page 10: Graduating cadets of the US Air Force Academy celebrate at their passing out ceremony, Colorado, 1966.

page 13: Five teachers hurdle a tennis net at the English-Scandinavian Summer School, Kent, UK, 1937.

page 14: Holiday makers in Jersey, 1933.

page 16: A boat flies over a ramp, at the Cypress Gardens speedboat race course in Florida, circa 1956.

page 19: Fencers June Paul and Raymond Paul during a fencing match, 1957.

page 21: Norwegian explorer Captain Roald Amundsen taking sights at the South Pole, 1911.

page 22: A passenger jumps to board a moving London bus, 1938.

page 25: Award winning sports photographer Reg Lancaster showing a runner crossing the finish line, the line itself on his nose, 1960.

page 26: Strongman Butty Sugroe uses his teeth to hold up Irish singer Bridie Gallagher on her chair, 1959.

page 28: "Pup of the Year" dachshund named Simon, with his trophy at London Zoo, 1979.

page 31: "Pushers" at work on Tokyo's Shinjuku station in the rush hour, circa 1970.

page 33: Stephen Hosgood, aged 8, winning a sack race at the Ravenor School Sports Day in Middlesex, UK, 1962.

page 35: A new arrival being initiated at a planting camp in the Nebraska Forest, 1914.

page 37: A man gives a woman a helping hand as she takes a flying leap over a large puddle, 1960.

page 39: A moutaineer reaches the summit of the Little Gelmerhorn in the Bernese Oberland, 1946.

page 40: Bjorn Borg in victory over John McEnroe at the Wimbledon Lawn Tennis Championships, 1980.

page 42: American actress Marilyn Monroe plays Amanda in the film "Let's Make Love," directed by George Cukor and produced by 20th Century Fox, 1960.

page 45: A waiter pours champagne into a tower of glasses to celebrate the opening of a new Casino at the Ritz Hotel, London, 1978.

page 47: A group of boys practice rescue tactics with an escape shute, 1943.-

page 48: Lifeguards on a Sydney beach in a balancing contest, 1931.

page 51: A girl twirls eight hula hoops simultaneously, circa 1965.

page 52: Mrs Powell watches her partner at the Women's Bowling Championships, Wimbledon, UK, 1973.

page 55: A man measuring the length of his waxed mustache, showing a span of fifteen inches, circa 1905, © R. Gates/Hulton Archive.

page 56: Circus strongman Paul Remos and his six and seven year old sons feeding a giraffe at London Zoo, circa 1950.

page 59: Lester Steers, American high jumper and world record holder for 12 years with a jump of 6 feet, 11 inches, circa 1945.

page 60: John McEnroe celebrates his victory over Bjorn Borg in the men's singles final at the Wimbledon Lawn Tennis Championships., 1981.

page 63: A little girl expresses her joy, 1946.

page 64: Studio image of a young girl smiling as she holds two dumbbell rattles over her head, circa 1955, © Lambert/Hulton Archive.

page 66: Andreas Dascher makes his winning jump at the International Ski Jumping Competition at St Moritz, 1947.

page 69: A construction worker at work on the water storage of a building in the City of London, 1956..

page 70: A man wearing metal thimbles and shooting electrical lightening from his fingertips, 1951.

page 73: A boy smiling as he hangs from the underside of a playground ladder, circa 1955.

page 74: A human cannonball flies through the air after being fired from a cannon, circa 1930.

page 77: A woman makes a splash as she lands on her back in the water, circa 1945, © William Rittases/Hulton Archive.

page 78: Sam Weaver of Chelsea FC, UK, leaps into the arms of his team-mates during a training session, 1939.

page 80: A workman demonstrating an escape panel which was fitted to the doors of American troopships in case they got jammed, 1944.

page 82: A group of girls jumping onto the beach, 1939.

page 84: Women walking along a palm tree, blown down by a hurricane on the island of Nassau, 1939.

page 87: Mary Johnson, the British cricketer who plays for York and England leaping at full stretch for a catch, 1951.

page 89: American actor Sidney Poitier holding his Best Actor Oscar for his performance in "Lilies of the Field," at the Academy Awards, Santa Monica, California, 1964, © Gene Lester/Archive Photos.

page 90: Aston Martin cars winning the top three places in the Tourist Trophy Sports Car Race at Goodwood, 1958.

page 93: American actor Irene Hervey receives a graduation diploma in the short comedy film, "A Thrill for Thelma", 1935.

page 94: Aerial acrobat Schindler, practicing one of his tricks from a Klemp plane piloted by Richard Perlia, circa 1927.

page 96: English skater Phil Taylor performing a daring leap over Freda Whitaker on the ice at St Moritz, circa 1930.

page 99: American singer and actor Nelson Eddy raising his arms in the air next to a palomino horse on the beach, circa 1938.

page 100: Speedway manager Johnny Hoskins jumping the net to congratulate Australian speedway rider "Bluey" Wilkinson, winner of their barefoot tennis match, 1937.

page 103: American actor Jack Lemmon (right) holds his Oscar for Best Supporting Actor in "Mister Roberts," pictured with American actor Burt Lancaster, at the Academy Awards, 1956.

page 104: Sailors from H.M.S. Fury on the beach in Jersey playing skipping with two female holiday makers, 1935.

page 107: American actor Kirk Douglas balances his son, Michael, aged three, on the soles of his feet, 1948.

page 109: American astronaut Edwin "Buzz" Aldrin, standing on the surface of the moon during the NASA Apollo 11 mission, 1969.

This edition published in 2002 by MQ Publications exclusively for Hallmark Cards, Inc.

www.hallmark.com

Printed and bound in China

2 3 4 5 6 7 8 9 10

Cover design: John Casey
Design: Alexia Smith
Text research: David Baird
Picture research: Suzie Green
Series Editor: Kate John